BAD FUR DAYS

By Gabrielle Tolliver

RUNNING PRESS
PHILADELPHIA · LONDON

9 8 7 6 5 4 3 2 1
Digit on the right indicates the number of this printing

Library of Congress Control Number: 2007937300

ISBN 978-0-7624-3086-4

Cover and interior design by Corinda Cook
Edited by Greg Jones
Typography: Antique Olive, Arial, Avenir, Caslon, Clarendon, Baileywick, Bank Gothic, Bodoni, Bordeaux, Bossa Nova, Calaban, Chicken Basket, Chowderhead, Congo, Copperplate, Dairyland, Dorchester Script, Ed, Goudy, Monotype Sorts, Optima, Rockwell, Runic, Sassoon, Stone Sans, TF Roux Borders, Tiki, Trade Gothic, and Typography of Coop

This book may be ordered by mail from the publisher. Please include $2.50 for postage and handling.
But try your bookstore first!

Running Press Book Publishers
2300 Chestnut Street
Philadelphia, Pennsylvania 19103-4371

Visit us on the web!
www.runningpress.com

WARNING: This book comes with a P-XXX rating, which means under no circumstance should you show it to your pet. The images of fur-do failure on the pages that follow are too extreme for safe viewing by sensitive animals. We strongly advise that you keep your copy of *Bad Fur Days* under lock and key and only take it out while your pet is napping or out in the yard chasing grasshoppers.

And, please, if you find that you dislike this book, resist the urge to tear out its pages and use them to line the litter box or dog cage. One glimpse of a photo—even a picture partially covered by cat litter or dog dirt—could cause your pet weeks of recurring nightmares and restless sleep. All that tossing and turning in bed would ensure that your pet endures many subsequent bad fur days. It might even lead to him or her ending up in the sequel. You have been advised.

YOU THINK YOU SUFFER THROUGH BAD HAIR DAYS?

Picture the case of "bed head" you'd wake up with each morning if you spent 18-hours-a-day in bed, like your typical feline does.

Imagine how often your 'do would come undone if you stuck your head out the window of a fast-moving car, the way your average dog does every chance he gets.

Or envision the daily dilemma faced by the offspring of a sleek dalmatian father and a longhaired Irish setter mother—with no access to a trimmer or color-correction products.

7

Just reading about it is probably enough to make your hair stand up on the back of your neck. (Or your fur, if you're a critter whose master didn't heed the warning above.) It should also help you appreciate why animals endure so many bad fur days. Not to mention a whole lot of bad feather, wool, mane, quill, and fin days. And let's not even get into all the social, emotional, professional, and dating disadvantages that a laughable lid brings with it.

8

Bad Fur Days celebrates these court jesters of the animal kingdom as they bravely battle bad fur-dos, fleas, shedding, bubble baths, fashion flubs, catastrophic coat markings, and all the accompanying woes. In the pages that follow, you'll find cats, dogs, llamas, birds, goats, rabbits, horses, simians and other animals coping with a coiffure crisis that would probably drive most humans to hide their heads beneath a baseball hat. Or a motorcycle helmet. Or under their bedspreads until they could arrange for an emergency house call from a hairstylist.

So give your love as well as your laughter for these courageous and hilarious critters. All animals deserve our kindness and respect—plus, when necessary, a quick brushing disguised as affectionate petting to straighten out their unfortunate 'dos and help them get through those bad fur days.

9

Devon realizes that she's overdone it again with the volumizing conditioner.

Ralph and Emma compare early morning cases of riverbed head.

Mario faces the fact that the Hitler mustache is on the "out" list—FOREVER!!

"Maybe my wife is right—it's time for an extreme makeover."

The three finalists
in the Equine
Fabio Lookalike
Contest vogue
one last time
for the judges.

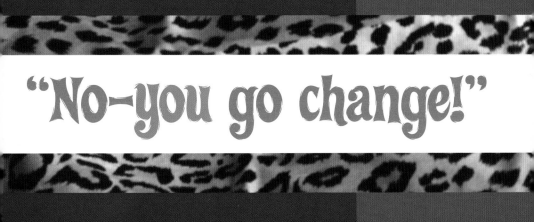

"No-you go change!"

Phyllis wonders if today is the day the '70s megafro finally comes back into vogue.

Shaun Cassidy tries to come to grips with his reincarnation.

"Lend me a talon, would you, Bert? My landing gear is stuck open again."

Little Gina vows that if she doesn't grow more fluffy and curvaceous by her next birthday, she's going to get wool implants.

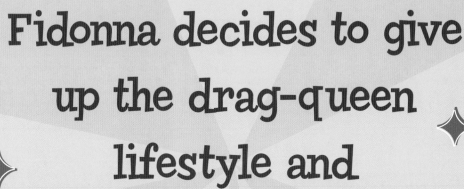

Fidonna decides to give up the drag-queen lifestyle and just go back to being plain ol' Fido.

SICK OF DOING CRUNCHES, LOU WONDERS IF HE CAN GET HIS STYLIST TO CORNROW A SIX-PACK AB PATTERN INTO HIS BELLY FUR.

Helen senses that her husband Harold is lying about how much he likes her new chartreuse highlights.

With the black spot on
his nose not responding
to acne creams,
Todd decides to consult
a furmatologist.

"And they call *me* a bitch."

Trevor confesses to his analyst that he believes he's the second coming of King Tut.

Gary ruins the family portrait by hacking up a furball.

Some days, no matter what you try, you just can't get your ear-do to work.

Tiffany bitchslaps Heather over her "blondes have more fleas" snipe.

**After breaking
an average
of six combs
per week
in his quills,
Woody goes
with a buzz cut.**

When all the prescription
powders and shampoos fail,
Martin turns to voodoo
to clear up his flea problem.

"Sure, I'm a little turned on. But he's really overdoing it with this macho plumage flexing."

Timmy tries to scare off the neighborhood tomcat by pretending he's turning into a miniature werewolf.

Joey gets caught "licking off."

Howard wonders if it's too late to cash in his money-back guarantee from Fur Club for Simians.

Louise hopes donkey designers soon replace "twig chic" with a more comfortable style of outerwear.

Kim displays the ill effects of getting only 14 hours of sleep per night instead of the recommended 19.

EVEN AFTER AN HOUR
OF COMBING, BLOW-DRYING,
AND MOUSSING,
BILL STILL CAN'T TEASE
HIS FUR OUT OF ITS
UNFLATTERING MIDDLE PART.

"I coulda' been a Kentucky Derby contender . . . if I coulda' seen my way into the starting gate."

With all the catnip gone,
Tony tries to liven up the party
with his imitation of Italy.

A cool breeze across his belly fur sends Rod into an embarrassing state of arousal during yoga class.

Barton stumbles home at dawn to face the wife after his drunken late-night trip to a tattoo parlor.

Sticking his head out of the window for the entire cross-country roadtrip fails to clear up Brock's dandruff.

Tina digests the news that *Vogue* just put cheetah skin on its Spring "out" list.

Leona feels much better since kicking her botox addiction, but looks so much worse.

Gwendolyn's innovative punk look nets her "Worst of Show" from the Westminster judges.

Gangland graffiti comes to farm country.

PETRA EMPLOYS BODY LANGUAGE TO FORM AN "F"—THE FIRST LETTER OF HER RESPONSE TO THE MASTER'S SUGGESTION THAT SHE TAKE A BATH.

"For the last time: it's a birthmark, not a bull's eye."

Reggie can't believe he let the

pushy salesman talk

him into installing fur siding

on his kitty condo.

89

TERRY GOES ON
THE LAM UNTIL
HER DISASTROUS
SPIRAL PERM
GROWS OUT.

Weary of all the primping required on the dog-show circuit, Jillian plots a move into the lapdog racket.

JABBA
THE
MUTT

94

Dwayne endures another round of lawn-ornament jokes from a group of rowdy bird watchers.

Trudi waits for her Brazilian Fur Straightening Treatment to wear off so she can fit her head back through the fence.

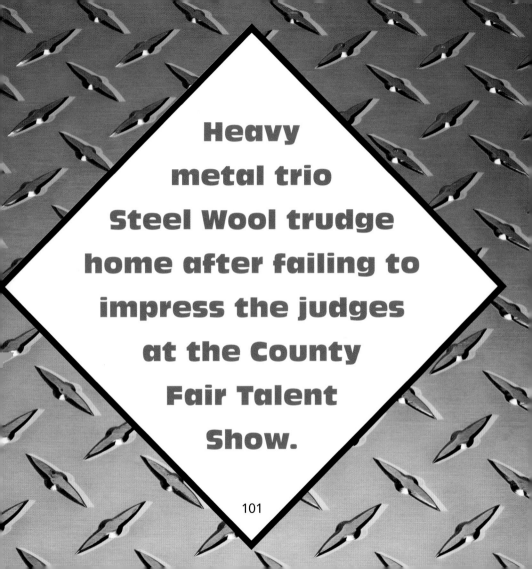

Heavy metal trio Steel Wool trudge home after failing to impress the judges at the County Fair Talent Show.

101

Rita storms off the set of the marine life documentary after the producers fail to meet her demands for a personal shell stylist.

Brenda decides to stop fighting the black-cat stigma and just go with it.

The B Street Bloodshots let the Lhasa Apso
know what they think of fancy,
long-haired breeds coming onto their turf.

Serge isn't fooling
anyone with
his new $5 toupee.

Mutt underdog Rocky Alpoa feels the sweat dripping down his fur as he arrives for his Frisbee Fetch title bout vs. longtime champ Apollo Pure Breed.

110

Former mob racehorse Wisey Jones tries to blend with the Wyoming cow herd he was placed into by the Federal Witness Protection Program.

Millie begins to suspect that there's a catch to Rancher Dan's free shape-and-trim offer.

After receiving nothing but laughing emoticons in response to his online personal ad, Ezekiel considers updating his look from Classic Amish.

Beth's new Britney Spears mane extensions fails to get her any play at the singles' trough.

Heddy worries that her pink furlights and jacket are too matchy-matchy.

"One more
Pepe Le Pew
crack, and
I'll headbutt
you in
the shins."

Sue realizes her stylist took her request for a "wedge cut" a little too literally.

IAN PERFORMS AT THE LOCAL KARAOKE BAR, TRYING TO RECAPTURE HIS GLORY DAYS IN THE 1980s BIG PLUMAGE BAND, A FLOCK OF PARROTS.

Butch vows to never again complain that the wind feels a little chilly on his bare fur.

EVEN WITH HIS NEW PAULIE WALNUTS HIGHLIGHTS, VITO CAN'T GAIN ENTRY INTO LA COSA NESTRA CRIME FLOCK.

Mildred serves as a  cautionary tale on the hazards of cutting your own bangs.

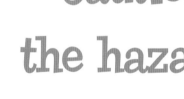

LEGENDARY FUR STYLIST VIDAL BABOON LAMENTS THE CANNIBALISM OUTBREAK CAUSED BY HIS NEW BANANA-SCENTED SHAMPOO FOR SIMIANS.

134

As he spots his mistress's foot coming toward him, Biff realizes that he's been mistaken for a bedroom slipper.

JEFF IS CRUSHED TO FIND OUT THAT HE'S ADOPTED.

With dismal reviews
and record-low ratings,
Magnum B.I.:
Lost Easter Egg Detective
gets canceled
after only one episode.

AFTER CATCHING HER
REFLECTION IN THE POND,
SHIRLEY CONCLUDES IT'S
TIME TO SPLURGE ON A
NEW PERM AND BEAK JOB.

Jake loses his street cred, watchdog job, and girlfriend within hours of unveiling his new jeri-curl perm.

Hank wonders if he has the right coloring to pull off his bird-hunting strategy of disguising himself as a weather vane.

Gil's ambitious scheme to ambush the Easter Bunny nets only a marshmallow mouse melted onto his fur.

Lily stares down the electrical outlet that just re-did her 'do.

Reginald dreams about turning into a giant storm cloud to circle the globe, raining on parades, picnics, and outdoor dog shows.

MORGAN CONNORS, PRESIDENT OF THE PRINCESS LEIA FAN CLUB FOR LEMURS.

Fifi has to laugh to keep from crying about her new mullet.

Hearing that horizontal stripes add 15 pounds to your ass, Shannon gallops to the mall to buy a pair of jeans.

Place your
favorite pet's
Bad Fur Day
photo here.

Look at my fabulous "do."